## Rhode Island Ecoregions

Northeastern Coastal Zone

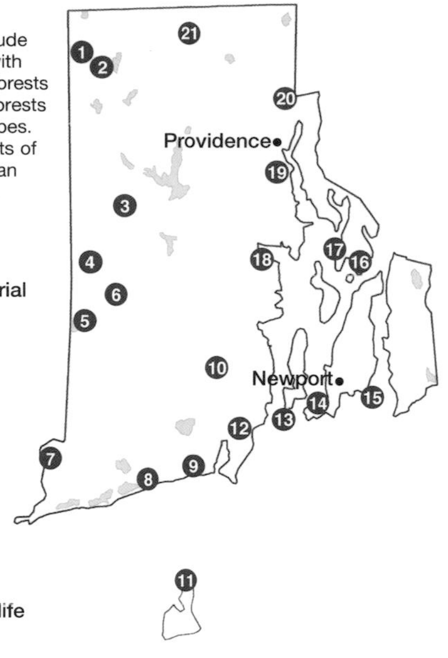


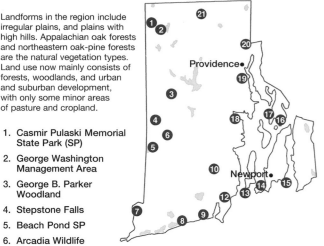

Landforms in the region include irregular plains, and plains with high hills. Appalachian oak forests and northeastern oak-pine forests are the natural vegetation types. Land use now mainly consists of forests, woodlands, and urban and suburban development, with only some minor areas of pasture and cropland.

1. Casmir Pulaski Memorial State Park (SP)
2. George Washington Management Area
3. George B. Parker Woodland
4. Stepstone Falls
5. Beach Pond SP
6. Arcadia Wildlife Management Area
7. Wilcox Park
8. Ninigret National Wildlife Refuge (NWR)
9. Trustom Pond NWR
10. University of Rhode Island Botanical Gardens
11. Block Island NWR
12. John H. Chafee NWR
13. Beavertail SP
14. Fort Adams SP
15. Sachuest Point NWR
16. Blithewold Mansion & Gardens
17. Colt State Park
18. Goddard Memorial SP
19. Roger Williams Park Botanical Center
20. Slater Mill Historic Garden
21. Richard Knight Fort Nature Refuge

Measurements denote the height of plants unless otherwise indicated. Illustrations are not to scale.

N.B. – Many edible wild plants have poisonous mimics. Never eat a wild plant or fruit unless you are absolutely sure it is safe to do so. The publisher makes no representation or warranties with respect to the accuracy, completeness, correctness or usefulness of this information and specifically disclaims any implied warranties of fitness for a particular purpose. The advice, strategies and/or techniques contained herein may not be suitable for all individuals. The publisher shall not be responsible for any physical harm (up to and including death), loss of profit or other commercial damage. The publisher assumes no liability brought or instituted by individuals or organizations arising out of or relating in any way to the application and/or use of the information, advice and strategies contained herein.

Waterford Press produces reference guides that introduce novices to nature, science, travel and languages. Product information is featured on the website: **www.waterfordpress.com**

Scan for more info

Made in the USA


To order, call 800-434-2555. For permissions, or to share comments, e-mail editor@waterfordpress.com. For information on custom-published products, call 800-434-2555 or e-mail info@waterfordpress.com.

ISBN 978-1-58355-516-3 $7.95 U.S.
9 781583 555163 50795
UPC 8 84682 01096 6
10 9 8 7 6 5 4 3 2 1 709237

RHODE ISLAND TREES & WILDFLOWERS – A Folding Pocket Guide to Familar Plants Kavanagh/Leung

A POCKET NATURALIST® GUIDE

# RHODE ISLAND TREES & WILDFLOWERS

A Folding Pocket Guide to Familar Plants

### Pitch Pine
*Pinus rigida* To 60 ft. (18 m)
Long needles grow in bundles of 3. Cone scales have stiff, curved spines. Bark is rich with resin (pitch).

### Eastern White Pine
*Pinus strobus* To 100 ft. (30 m)
Needles grow in bundles of 5. Cone is up to 8 in. (20 cm) long.

### Eastern Redcedar
*Juniperus virginiana* To 60 ft. (18 m)
4-sided branchlets are covered with overlapping, scale-like leaves. Fruit is a blue berry.

### Trembling Aspen
*Populus tremuloides* To 70 ft. (21 m)
Long-stemmed leaves rustle in the slightest breeze. The most widely distributed tree in North America.

### Yellow Poplar (Tuliptree)
*Liriodendron tulipifera* To 120 ft. (36.5 m)
Note unusual leaf shape. Showy flowers are succeeded by cone-like aggregates of papery, winged seeds.

### American Elm
*Ulmus americana* To 100 ft. (30 m)
Note vase-shaped profile. Leaves are toothed. Fruits have a papery collar and are notched at the tip.

### Black Willow
*Salix nigra* To 100 ft. (30 m)
Tree or shrub, often leaning. Slender leaves are shiny green on the upper surface. Flowers bloom in long, fuzzy clusters.

### Boxelder
*Acer negundo* To 60 ft. (18 m)
Leaves have 3-7 leaflets. Seeds are encased in paired papery keys.

### Sugar Maple
*Acer saccharum* To 100 ft. (30 m)
Leaves have five coarsely-toothed lobes. Fruit is a winged seed pair. Tree sap is the source of maple syrup.

### Red Maple
*Acer rubrum* To 90 ft. (27 m)
Leaves have 3-5 lobes and turn scarlet in autumn. Flowers are succeeded by red, winged seed pairs. **Rhode Island's state tree.**

### Paper Birch
*Betula papyrifera* To 70 ft. (21 m)
Whitish bark peels off trunk in thin sheets. Bark was used by Native Americans to make bowls and canoes.

### Black Birch
*Betula lenta* To 80 ft. (24 m)
Leaves are saw-toothed. Twigs smell like wintergreen. Dark bark is brown to blackish.



### Yellow Birch
*Betula alleghaniensis*
To 100 ft. (30 m)
Bark is red to yellowish and peels off in strips. Cone-like oval fruit grows erect on branchlets.

### Common Chokecherry
*Prunus virginiana* To 20 ft. (6 m)
Cylindrical clusters of spring flowers are succeeded by dark, red-purple berries.

### American Beech
*Fagus grandifolia* To 80 ft. (24 m)
Flowers bloom in rounded clusters in spring and are succeeded by 3-sided nuts.

### Flowering Dogwood
*Cornus florida* To 30 ft. (9 m)
Tiny yellow flowers bloom in crowded clusters surrounded by 4 white petal-like structures.

### White Oak
*Quercus alba* To 100 ft. (30 m)
Leaves have 5-9 rounded lobes. Acorn has a shallow, scaly cup.

### Scarlet Oak
*Quercus coccinea* To 80 ft. (24 m)
Leaves have 7-9 spreading lobes and are up to 7 in. (18 cm) long. Leaves turn scarlet in fall.

### Black Oak
*Quercus velutina* To 80 ft. (24 m)
Leaves have 5-7 spiny lobes. Acorns have a ragged-edged cup.

### Beaked Hazelnut
*Corylus cornuta* To 10 ft. (3 m)
Sheathed, nut-like fruit matures into edible filberts by autumn.

### Bitternut Hickory
*Carya cordiformis* To 80 ft. (24 m)
Leaves have 7-11 leaflets. Twigs end in yellow buds. Bitter fruits are unpalatable to most wildlife.

### Mockernut Hickory
*Carya tomentosa* To 80 ft. (24 m)
Rounded, thick-shelled fruits have 4 prominent grooves. Fruits are sweet.

### Hackberry
*Celtis occidentalis* To 90 ft. (27 m)
Leaves are slightly toothed and curved at the tip. Red to purple fruits grow singly at the end of long stems.

### American Sycamore
*Platanus occidentalis* To 100 ft. (30 m)
Leaves have 3-5 shallow lobes. Rounded fruits are bristly.



### Green Ash
*Fraxinus pennsylvanica* To 60 ft. (18 m)
Leaves have 7-9 leaflets. Flowers are succeeded by single-winged fruits.

### Sassafras
*Sassafras albidum* To 60 ft. (18 m)
Aromatic tree or shrub has leaves that are mitten-shaped or 3-lobed. Fruits are dark berries.

### Black Cherry
*Prunus serotina* To 80 ft. (24 m)
Aromatic bark and leaves smell cherry-like. Dark berries have an oval stone inside.

### Witch Hazel
*Hamamelis virginiana* To 30 ft. (9 m)
Shrub or small tree. Tiny yellow flowers bloom along leafless twigs in the fall. Woody fruits eject their seeds when ripe.

### Black Tupelo
*Nyssa sylvatica* To 100 ft. (30 m)
Crown has horizontal branches. Glossy leaves turn red in autumn. Blue fruits have ridged seeds.

### Black Walnut
*Juglans nigra* To 90 ft. (27 m)
Leaves have 9-23 leaflets. Greenish fruits have a black nut inside.

### American Basswood
*Tilia americana* To 100 ft. (30 m)
Leaves are heart-shaped. Flowers and nutlets hang from narrow leafy bracts. Often multi-trunked.

### Eastern Hophornbeam
*Ostrya virginiana* To 50 ft. (15 m)
Trunk has sinewy, muscle-like bark. Hop-like fruits are hanging, cone-like clusters.

### Pin Cherry
*Prunus pensylvanica* To 30 ft. (9 m)
Lance-shaped leaves have curled margins. Small clusters of whitish flowers are succeeded by bright red berries.

### American Holly
*Ilex opaca* To 70 ft. (21 m)
Tree or shrub is distinguished by its stiff, spiny evergreen leaves and red, poisonous berries.

### Common Juniper
*Juniperus communis* To 4 ft. (1.2 m)
Needle-like leaves grow in whorls of 3 around twigs. Berry-like, blue-black cones have 1-3 seeds.

### Common Serviceberry
*Amelanchier arborea* To 40 ft. (12 m)
White, star-shaped flowers bloom early in spring. Red to purple-black berries ripen in mid-summer.



### Smooth Sumac
*Rhus glabra* To 20 ft. (6 m)
Clusters of white flowers are succeeded by 'hairy' red fruits. Bark is gray and smooth.

### Lowbush Blueberry
*Vaccinium angustifolium*
To 2 ft. (60 cm)
A low mat-forming shrub.

### Virginia Creeper
*Parthenocissus quinquefolia*
Vines to 150 ft. (45 m) long. Climbing vine. Leaves turn brilliant red in fall. Small, dark fruits are poisonous.

### Kinnikinnick
*Arctostaphylos uva-ursi*
To 12 in. (30 cm)
Pinkish, bell-shaped flowers are succeeded by red-orange, mealy berries. Also known as bearberry.

### American Elder
*Sambucus canadensis*
To 16 ft. (4.8 cm)
Shrub or small tree. Saw-toothed leaves have 3-7 leaflets. Flowers are succeeded by dark berries.

### Eastern Poison Ivy
*Toxicodendron radicans*
To 8 ft. (2.4 m)
Flowers bloom in loose clusters. Three-part leaves turn red in autumn.

### Large Cranberry
*Vaccinium macrocarpon*
To 12 in. (30 cm)
Creeping shrub is found in boggy areas and is also grown commercially.

### Northern Arrowwood
*Viburnum recognitum*
To 15 ft. (4.5 m)
Thicket-forming shrub has white flowers and blue berries. One of the most common woody plants in the state.

### Mountain Laurel
*Kalmia latifolia* To 20 ft. (6 m)
Evergreen shrub or small tree. Leaves are leathery.

### Blackberry
*Rubus allegheniensis*
To 10 ft. (3 m)
Leaves usually have 3 leaflets. White flowers are succeeded by red berries that blacken when ripe.

### Steeplebush
*Spiraea tomentosa*
To 4 ft. (1.2 m)

### Wild Red Raspberry
*Rubus idaeus*
To 6 ft. (1.8 m)
Leaves have 3-5 leaflets. Fruits appear in summer.

### Buttonbush
*Cephalanthus occidentalis*
To 10 ft. (3 m)
'Pincushion' flowers have protruding stamens.

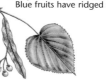

**Bloodroot**
*Sanguinaria canadensis*
To 10 in. (25 cm)
Root has a reddish sap.

**Jack-in-the-Pulpit**
*Arisaema* spp.
To 3 ft. (90 cm)
Club-like stem is
surrounded by a curving,
green to purplish hood.

**Wood Anemone**
*Anemone quinquefolia*
To 8 in. (20 cm)
Found in moist
meadows and woods.

**Shinleaf**
*Pyrola rotundifolia*
To 8 in. (20 cm)
Waxy white flowers
are very fragrant.

**Nodding Ladys' Tresses**
*Spiranthes cernua*
To 2 ft. (60 cm)
Flowers bloom in spiral
rows on flower stalk.

**Indian Pipe**
*Monotropa uniflora*
To 10 in. (25 cm)
Waxy white plant is
parasitic on other
plants in shady
woods.

**Dutchman's Breeches**
*Dicentra cucullaria*
To 12 in. (30 cm)
Spurred flowers
resemble trousers.

**Wild Calla**
*Calla palustris*
To 3 ft. (90 cm)
Tiny green flowers are
surrounded by a showy
white spathe.

**Queen Anne's Lace**
*Daucus carota*
To 4 ft. (1.2 m)
Flower clusters become
cup-shaped as they age.

**Canada Mayflower**
*Maianthemum canadense*
To 6 in. (15 cm)
Star-shaped flowers bloom
in a spire-like cluster.

**Oxeye Daisy**
*Leucanthemum vulgare*
To 3 ft. (90 cm)
Showy flowers bloom
along roadsides
in summer.

**Swamp Azalea**
*Rhododendron
viscosum*
To 10 ft. (3 m)

**Leatherleaf**
*Chamaedaphne calyculata*
To 4 ft. (1.2 m)
Leathery leaves have
rolled edges.

**Sweet White Violet**
*Viola blanda*
To 5 in. (13 cm)

**Solomon's Zigzag**
*Maianthemum racemosum*
To 5 ft. (1.5 m)
Tiny flowers bloom
in a dense terminal
cluster and are
succeeded by red
berries. Note
kinked stem.

**White Baneberry**
*Actaea pachypoda*
To 3 ft. (90 cm)
Poisonous white berries
have a black dot. Also
called doll's eyes

**Wild Strawberry**
*Fragaria virginiana*
Stems to 8 in. (20 cm)
Creeping plant has
5-petalled flowers
that are succeeded
by the familiar fruit.

**Starflower**
*Trientalis borealis*
To 8 in. (20 cm)

**Fragrant Water Lily**
*Nymphaea odorata*
Flower to 6 in.
(15 cm) wide.

**Yellow Flag**
*Iris pseudacorus*
To 3 ft. (90 cm)

**Butterfly Weed**
*Asclepias tuberosa*
To 3 ft. (90 cm)
Orange flowers
are star-shaped.

**Lousewort**
*Pedicularis canadensis*
To 18 in. (45 cm)
'Snapdragon' flowers
may be yellow to red.

**Seaside Goldenrod**
*Solidago
sempervirens*
To 8 ft. (2.4 m)
Grows in sandy soil
and salt marshes.

**Yellow Lady's Slipper**
*Cypripedium calceolus*
To 28 in. (70 cm)

**Turk's Cap Lily**
*Lilium superbum*
To 7 ft. (2.1 m)

**Wood Lily**
*Lilium philadelphicum*
To 28 in. (70 cm)

**Butter-and-Eggs**
*Linaria vulgaris*
To 3 ft. (90 cm)
Spurred flowers
have a patch of
orange in the
throat.

**Goldenrod**
*Solidago* spp.
To 5 ft. (1.5 m)
Flowers bloom in
arched clusters.

**Buttercup**
*Ranunculus* spp.
To 3 ft. (90 cm)
Flower petals are
waxy to the touch.

**Marsh Marigold**
*Caltha palustris*
To 2 ft. (60 cm)
Aquatic plant has
large, heart-shaped
leaves.

**Common Sunflower**
*Helianthus* spp.
To 9 ft. (2.7 m)
Flowers follow the sun
across the sky each day.

**Yellow Pond Lily**
*Nuphar* spp.
Flower to 2.5 in.
(6 cm) wide.
Floating aquatic plant.

**Black-eyed Susan**
*Rudbeckia hirta*
To 3 ft. (90 cm)
Flower has a dark,
conical central disk.

**Jewelweed**
*Impatiens capensis*
To 5 ft. (1.5 m)
Spotted, orange-yellow
flowers are horn-shaped.
Ripe seed capsules
burst when touched.

**Yellow Wild Indigo**
*Baptisia tinctoria*
To 3 ft. (90 cm)

**Limber Honeysuckle**
*Lonicera dioica*
To 7 ft. (2.1 m)
Grows in sandy soil.

**Evening Primrose**
*Oenothera* spp.
To 5 ft. (1.5 m)
Lemon-scented,
4-petalled flowers
bloom in the evening.

**Dogtooth Violet**
*Erythronium americanum*
To 10 in. (25 cm)
Common in meadows
and rich woodlands.

**Yellow Violet**
*Viola* spp.
To 12 in. (30 cm)
Flowers have dark
veins on 3 of 5 petals.

**Cardinal Flower**
*Lobelia cardinalis*
To 4 ft. (1.2 m)

**Pink Lady's Slipper**
*Cypripedium acaule*
To 14 in. (35 cm)

**Blazing Star**
*Liatris scariosa*
To 5 ft. (1.5 m)

**Rose Pogonia**
*Pogonia
ophioglossoides*
To 2 ft. (60 cm)

**Beach Pea**
*Lathyrus japonicus*
To 2 ft. (60 cm)
Creeping plant
found on dunes
and beaches.

**Gaywings**
*Polygala paucifolia*
To 7 in. (18 cm)
Flower has 2
large 'wings'.

**Trailing Arbutus**
*Epigaea repens*
Stems to 16 in. (40 cm)
Creeping plant has pink
or white flowers.

**Wild Geranium**
*Geranium maculatum*
To 2 ft. (60 cm)

**Rhododendron**
*Rhododendron maximum*
To 35 ft. (10.7 m)
Flowering shrub has
white to pinkish flowers.

**Crimson-eyed Rosemallow**
*Hibiscus palustris*
To 6 ft. (1.8 m)

**Wild Ginger**
*Asarum canadense*
To 12 in. (30 cm)
Flowers arise at base
of 2 leaves.

**Columbine**
*Aquilegia canadensis*
To 2 ft. (60 cm)

**Wild Rose**
*Rosa carolina*
To 3 ft. (90 cm)

**Grass Pink**
*Calopogon* spp.
To 20 in. (50 cm)
Plant has a single
grass-like leaf.

**Russian Thistle**
*Salsola kali*
To 3 ft. (90 cm)
Invasive
seashore weed.

**Twinflower**
*Linnaea borealis*
To 4 in. (10 cm)
Flowers bloom in
nodding pairs.

**Virginia Meadow Beauty**
*Rhexia virginica*
To 2 ft. (60 cm)
Pink flowers have
8 yellow stamens.

**Rose Azalea**
*Rhododendron roseum*
To 9 ft. (2.7 m)

**Milkweed**
*Asclepias* spp.
To 4 ft. (1.2 m)
Leaves and stem
are sticky.

**Red Trillium**
*Trillium erectum*
To 16 in. (40 cm)
Flowers smell of rotting
flesh. Also known as
stinking Benjamin.

**Bluets**
*Houstonia caerulea*
To 6 in. (15 cm)
Yellow-centered flowers
grow in large colonies.

**New England Aster**
*Aster novae-angliae*
To 7 ft. (2.1 m)

**Fringed Gentian**
*Gentianopsis crinita*
To 3 ft. (90 cm)

**Harebell**
*Campanula
rotundifolia*
To 40 in. (1 m)

**Skunk Cabbage**
*Symplocarpus foetidus*
To 2 ft. (60 cm)
Plant exudes a foetid
odor that attracts insects.

**Common Blue Violet**
*Viola sororia*
To 8 in. (20 cm)
**Rhode Island's
state flower.**

**Blue Flag**
*Iris versicolor*
To 3 ft. (90 cm)

**Northern Pitcher Plant**
*Sarracenia purpurea*
To 2 ft. (60 cm)
Carnivorous plant has
cup-shaped leaves
that trap insects.

**Chicory**
*Cichorium intybus*
To 6 ft. (1.8 m)
Wheel-shaped
flowers are varying
shades of blue.

**Purple Loosestrife**
*Lythrum salicaria*
To 7 ft. (2.1 m)
Invasive weed is
very common in
marshes and
ponds.

**Blue-eyed Grass**
*Sisyrinchium
angustifolium*
To 20 in. (50 cm)

**Wild Blue Lupine**
*Lupinus perennis*
To 2 ft. (60 cm)
Note star-shaped leaves.

**Birdfoot Violet**
*Viola pedata*
To 10 in. (25 cm)
Leaves are birdfoot-
shaped.

**Wild Bergamot**
*Monarda fistulosa*
To 4 ft. (1.2 m)

**Sea Lavender**
*Limonium
carolinianum*
To 2 ft. (60 cm)
Coastal plant.

**Asiatic Dayflower**
*Commelina communis*
To 3 ft. (90 cm)
Flowers have two
large blue petals
above a tiny
white one.

**Blueweed**
*Echium vulgare*
To 30 in. (75 cm)
Blue flowers have
long, red stamens.
Also called viper's
bugloss. Invasive.

**Pickerelweed**
*Pontederia cordata*
To 4 ft. (1.2 m)
Aquatic plant.

**Bittersweet Nightshade**
*Solanum dulcamara*
Vine to 10 ft. (3 m) long.
Purplish flowers
have a yellow 'beak'.

**Joe-Pye Weed**
*Eupatorium* spp.
To 7 ft. (2.1 m)
Flowers are pink to
purple. Leaves grow in
whorls of 3-5.

**Cow Vetch**
*Vicia cracca*
Stems to 7 ft.
(2.1 m) long.

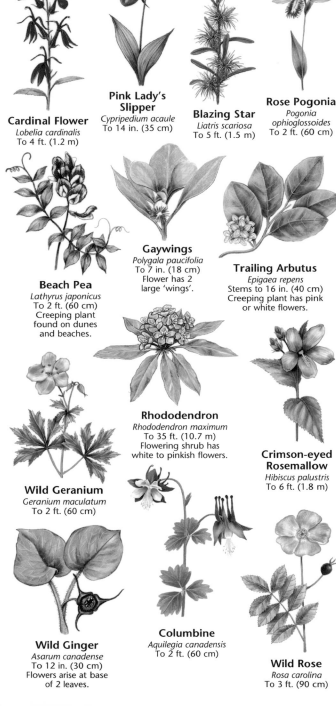

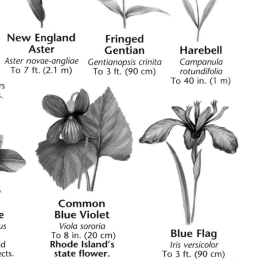

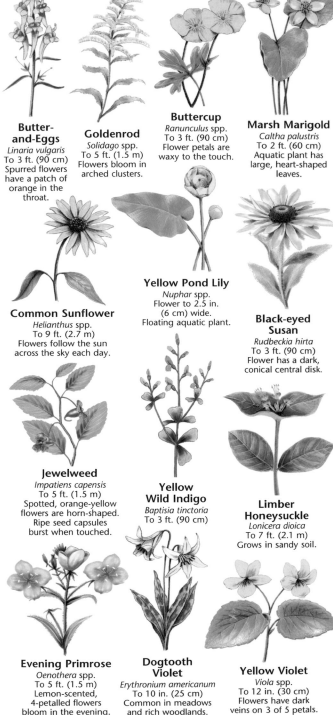
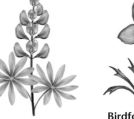
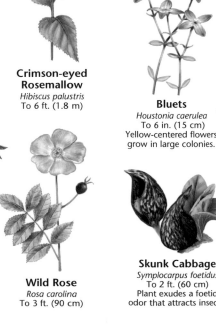

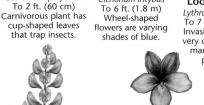
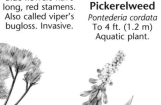
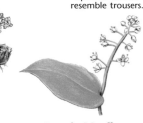
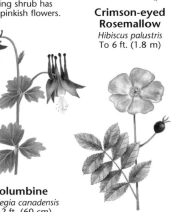

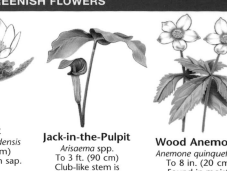